Deliriously Unapologetic

Deliriously Unapologetic

*Not Apologizing For Being Me
Transparency In My Own Poetic Form*

SHELIAH M. CALLAHAN

LUMINARE PRESS
WWW.LUMINAREPRESS.COM

Deliriously Unapologetic: Not Apologizing For Being Me
Transparency In My Own Poetic Form
Copyright © 2024 by Sheliah M. Callahan

All rights reserved. This book or any portion thereof may not be reproduced or used in any manner whatsoever without the express written permission of the author, except for the use of brief quotations in a book review.

Printed in the United States of America

Illustration @csaimages

Luminare Press
442 Charnelton St.
Eugene, OR 97401
www.luminarepress.com

LCCN: 2024911333
ISBN: 979-8-88679-587-5

This book of poems is dedicated to all the delirious people who continue to survive and embrace life in spite of...

*Delirious—Out of one's senses,
intoxicated, and wildly excited*

Delirious

Delirious I am,
at times having complete
control, but other times I
just let go, erratic or not,
it's me doing what I do best
and to some degree, I find
peace in not following anyone's
lead, or trying to adhere to what
is suppose to be, and to others I
may seem irrational because I
refuse to do what is so called
acceptable, and for all these things
I'm unapologetic,

I'm living in my truth, just
being me, and crying when
I want to, and feeling not only
for me, but for you too, and then
there're times I say what's on my
mind, blunt as it may be, it's me
asserting myself after years of
stifling, you see, I walk to my own
beat, created and cultivated to suit
me, but then there're times, as scary
as it may be, I unleash this rage that
overcomes me, with bouts of
screaming and laughing,

simultaneously, oh what a
sight to see, but maybe it's
because of society's pressures,
or simply what I place upon me,

and lets not talk about that
one love, that will take you
over, the one that you hung
on to far too long, but seeing
past imperfections, and deep
rooted wounds, but then there
are times I just go with the
flow and let things settle,
marinate, and just let it be

I make no excuses, for I
know all these ups and downs
are what make me, embracing
my whole being—
Delirious I am,
but apologetic I'm
not, and will never be

Contents

Mood/Love 1
Strength 49
Survival 85

Acknowledgements 115
About the Author 117

It's the giving, my heart
the releasing, my soul
the trusting, my fear

Mood/Love

Love Letters

From me to him:

I want him to heal from the inside out,
I want him to have peace, to embrace
each day, and roll with whatever
comes his way, I want him to
not only know, but to feel his
worth

I want him to realize that money
doesn't define success, it can't
even buy happiness, but it
does come in the smallest
packages, for I want him
to know that above
anything, love is
what wins in the
end, love is what
holds everything,
I mean everything together,
unconditional
S.C.

From him to me:

"I want her to know that what I
feel for her is beyond Love,
that when I think of her
I feel her in a way I cannot
explain——only that the
very thought of her is to

experience what love is
meant to be, that
which had no word,
but just is……."
                    V.I.

My Kind of Love

My kind of love is unspoken, it's that
feeling I get, kind of like when you're
floating, that tingling inside when
everything's flowing, it's me putting
my life on the line, about to burn and
explode inside, kind of crazy, and feeling
delirious most of the time, you see the
love that I feel, keeps me warm inside,
wrapped like a cocoon, protected
inside, it even makes my food
taste better each and every time,
it's that kind of love that makes
me want to scream and savor
inside, it's my kind of love
that makes me feel
whole inside

Reminiscing

I wonder when night falls,
does he think of me at all,
does he reminisce of our
hearts beating as one,
intertwined, and held
in each other's arms

Does he miss my scent,
and how we looked at
each another, as if
there were no other

I wonder as night falls,
does he keep a special
place for us close to
his heart, that connection,
that could never be
mistaken, broken,
or torn apart

I wonder as night falls,
as I lay surrendered and
open, do his thoughts
rest upon me before he
lays himself down
to sleep

Sheliah M. Callahan

I wonder
will I forever be embedded
in his mind, and a part of
his soul, that sacred place
that could never be denied,
or replaced

Crushing on You

You move me in every way
it's kind of hard to say, just
how one look makes me feel
this way, like summer on a
cold winter day, melting like
chocolate every time you
come around my way

Broken

Spewing daggers,
piercing, and harsh,
unrelenting, and
cutting straight
through to my
heart

Lost

I sacrificed my whole existence for you,
losing myself, the person I use to be,
just to be present, seen, and loved
by you

Vow

When you finally left, and never looked back,
I knew it was my time to finally let go, let go
of that false hope of building a home, a
sanctuary where nothing could come
between us, separate us, or break
our bond that we......
you remember that vow of eternity

Lonely Nights

It's nights like these,
when loneliness sets
in, the past surfacing
once again, finding
a way to remain, as
it takes over, leaving
me no peace, just
pain

Intuition

It's like I'm on this high,
shaking on the inside,
about to explode, and
not quite understanding
this strong hold, and
although I can't clearly
see whats before me,
I'm going with how
I feel like my mama
told me

The Other Woman

I thought you were fine,
I thought you were mine,
at least until a quarter
past nine

Dysfunctional Relationship

Knock, knock,
here we go again, knocking at my door,
telling myself no not this time as I'm
pacing across the floor, sweaty palms,
shallow breath, feeling depleted as I
chant I will be stronger this time, and
not allow you to come back in, at
least not this time

Racing thoughts,

Should I give in, not give in, give this
a second chance, or is this the fifth,
losing count of this tumultuous past,
and at one time I thought it was
suppose to be, showcasing my
love, and dedication for all to see,
a picture perfect scene, but not
quite how it turned out to be,
roses, and sweet talking was the
routine, every time I tried to leave

Racing thoughts,

I will be stronger this time, resisting
this temptation, a snake in disguise,
slithering in and out, as I'm fighting
to stay alive, and feeling caved in,
in a tunnel echoing my bellowing cries,
as I desperately try to find my way out

Am I NOT ENOUGH-

Am I NOT ENOUGH-

Hearing the echos of my pleas within me,
sunken to the ground,

Am I NOT ENOUGH-

As I let it all go, feeling defeated, and closed
in, and slowly dissolving to never resurface again

To Know Me

I have to remind myself that I have
the highest of the high instilled in
me, as I salute, trumpets ringing
in my ear, and all around me, for
I have royalty running through
me, to know me, is to love
me, and to love me, is to
understand, and accept
everything about me

Acceptance

Forgive me,
for loving
myself

Simple Days

A simple day for me is letting tomorrow rest where it may, thoughts fading away, no longer resting or nestling, trying to block my way

A simple day for me is sometimes being into me, taking care of me from the inside out, and flushing out all the impurities that once tried to overtake me

A simple day for me is laughter, and enjoying, and loving all those around me

A simple day for me is looking at all the beauty surrounding me, as the sunlight beats down on me, arms spread wide, looking up at the sky, and feeling free, amazing, and thankful for simple days like these

Feeling Blessed

I never realized all the beauty bestowed upon
me until life slowed me down, and my senses
became heightened, as if I was experiencing life
for the first time, from the cool grass beneath
my feet, to the humming birds whisking by,
to the mountains touching the sky, and just
the pure laughter of children playing near
by, their innocence, and joy dancing in the
air, shades galore, their beauty exquisite,
and shining through, multi-cultural, a
perfect rainbow, inhaling it all, and
not asking to be anywhere, but here,
surrounded, and feeling full

Reclaiming Myself

Each day I'm falling deeper in love
with who I am, and who I've become,
as I struggled with how to accept and
love, after years of being broken,
and having to pick up the pieces,
and not quite knowing where to
begin, until that day when I realized
it was never me, and I truly saw
and was in awe of all that I
possessed in me, becoming in
love all over again with every part
of me, and simply putting me first,
allowing my beauty to shine through,
and illuminate the room, so powerful,
and unable to restrain, creating this
strength and peace from within,
allowing me to be open again,
and to never allow another to
steal my joy, or take away
that love I fought so hard
to reclaim

Vibes

Greetings,
as the sun rises,
dew drops slowly
disappearing on my
window pane, clearing
my way as I look on,
feeling the vibes of
this day

Solace

Aliso, Aliso take me away,
erasing the day so I can
play, as the sand beneath
my feet gives way, my
imprints slowly washed
away, but as steady as
I could be, I took in
that cool summer
breeze, as the warm
sunset caressed me,
and those waves,
gravitated,
manipulated, and,
hypnotized me

Mood

Something about sunsets and
warm summer nights

On My Way Home

I'm on my way home, memories held wherever I go,
just the feeling alone is all that it takes when the aroma
greets me at the front door, taking me back to my
childhood, a kid again, playing all day, and hair
going every which way, just the mere excitement
of music in the air, seeming like miles away as
all the children waited impatiently while dancing
in the streets from the heat scorching their feet
as we lined up to the best tasting ice cream in
town, gripping it tightly as it dripped, and
zigzagged its way down, sticky and all,
and not a care in the world, just innocence
in the air, as beads of sweat traveled down
our faces, sun beaming, and shining
down on us, giving us grace and
watching over us

I'm on my way home, a place that I hold,
and just the feeling alone is all that it
takes, to make me feel completed,
and whole

Friday Nights

Friday nights, flashing lights,
leaving my worries and week
behind, while feeling that beat
and swaying my hips until the
sun comes back around

Blue Skies

It's funny how the color blue transforms to be whatever you want it to, creating that mood, whether it's gloomy or just making you feel some type of way on any given day, or at times feeling there's no way out, no refuge, but for me, when I think of blues, I see blue skies that brighten my way, blue jays flying graciously above, wings spread wide, and the possibilities beyond measure, it's like that feeling of life, being reborn, just the beauty alone transforms
me and sets this mood, putting me at
peace, surrendering, and finally
feeling free,
mind,
body,
and soul

Grateful

I'm grateful for existing,
feeling, and just being

The Beauty in <u>You</u>

Have you ever listened to a song, and hung on to every note, the highs and the lows, as if it came from you, inside you, capturing your past and taking you back, a part that you could never tap into, that tugged at you, and as the notes played, this feeling brewed, and stirred inside you, allowing you to finally see the beauty in you, and all that has made you

Delicately Made

One of a kind,
created and molded,
and delicately made,
to be handled with
care, and to never
be compared

Wings

A love lost, but never forgotten,
replaying our past like a broken
record, back in my days on a
Friday night, girlfriends around
and crying all night, like the world
was ending, or caving in, pure
numbness setting in, then
realization starts kicking in,
and no longer holding me
back again, for young love
was not meant to last
forever, as we spread
our wings to find another

Letting Go

Loving you,
is letting go,
so you will
grow

Not Sorry

This is me, all of me,
nothing more, nothing
less, just me being
who I was meant
to be

Blinded

Blinded and shielded
I could not see,
the destruction,
and plotting
surrounding me

Gray Skies

Catching me on a particular
day or time, may not be wise
when there're gray skies

Holding On

Savoring this moment as if it's our last,
not wanting to let go, afraid you'll
vanish and be erased from my past,
or become this distant memory as
I struggle to hold on, wanting to
freeze that moment in time, after
dusk and before sun comes, and
to feel everything you were
giving and me releasing all
that I had, intertwined and
moving, beating as one, it's
like envisioning that wave,
embodying that moment, in
sync with that flow, and riding
it through until the tide subsides,
it's a high like no other, a
memory captured and ingrained
forever, savoring that moment,
as if it's our last

Sheliah M. Callahan

Secured

Whisper to me just one more time
of how my undying love, my sweet
scent, and just one look, mesmerized,
captivated, and secured your love

Heartache

Even apart, I feel every part of you,
like our souls are connected, like it
was meant to be, but at times it
becomes unbearable, a yearning
like no other, as I fight to contain
my feelings that took root the
first day I laid eyes on you,
but now I weep, and pray
that there will be a day
when all this will fade,
like a vision of the
past, an Illusion
that vanishes in
a smoke filled
room

Alone You Stand

Have you ever been in love,
but love didn't have your back?
given all you could, but left you
where you stood, sacrificing, and
not realizing, it never existed,
never surfaced, or even bloomed,
like a seed never taken root, or
like summer, without the soothing
waters refreshing you, and making
you feel anew, or winter without a
warm touch, making you want more,
yearning for what is physically
not there, or even awakening to realize
it was only a dream, but your feelings
remained, never changed, and never
wavered, knowing it was only you
giving this love, as you were left
where you stood, as if you were
the one that never existed

Awakening

Goodbyes are never easy, especially
if you're the one that's refusing to
let go, tearing yourself inside out,
and questioning why, or simply
wondering how to remain sane,
while realizing you were deeper
involved than you let on, not only
to others, and to the world, but
to the one torn—
Yourself

Moved On

The realization that it is
over, when his fixation
is on another

Searching

Sometimes I ask myself if I can do this in and
out thing before going to sleep and not knowing
what tomorrow will bring, there are times I
wish I could freeze certain moments in time,
locking it in and repeating the same day
over and over again, for me when it's
good it puts me on this high, it's like
reaching a peak that has me feeling
good inside, screaming inside, and
making me wanna dance inside

My Soulmate

When my day shifts
not quite the way
I want it to, I think
of you to get me
through

Brighter Days

Rainbows remind me of brighter days
to come, filled with hope, and that
calming feeling that everything
will fall into place,
that comfort zone
that feel good zone
that all inclusive zone,
and that zone where nothing
overshadows, but lets you shine as
you are

Distant Memory

Like the fields in the fall,
withered and worn,
scorched and brittle,
this distant memory
will forever be etched
in my mind, me running
through the fields laughing
and playing, hiding and
seeking from sun up to
sun down, and not a
care in the world,
just me being me,
and relishing in
those times with
the ones dear
to me

Restored

Running as fast as you can to catch that chance,
to make you over again, receiving what you
could not see so long ago, oh how it could
have saved you, restored you, and made
you whole

I'm still standing, I'm still rising
I'm still here

Strength

I choose

I choose, to uncover me,
layers upon layers that
weighted me, holding me
down, and trying to
overtake me

I choose, to not let you
smoother me, or stifle my
every move, as I step high,
and landing with the strength of
my mother, crushing all the negativity

I choose, to live my way, not caring
what others say

I choose, to be seen in the light that
comes from me, not the darkness lurking
around corners trying to suck the
life out of me

I choose, peace and tranquility,
harmony all around me

I choose,

I choose,

In spite of…I choose

She Stood

She stood,
with all the strength she had,

She stood,
with all the burden she carried,

She stood,
with all the pain she felt,

She stood,
with all the love she had,

She stood,
with all her might

She Stood……

Finding Me

She ran,
and never
looked back,
holding on to
what she had,
that light that
was gone
came back

She ran,
restored,
renewed,
a newfound
sense of what
she truly
possessed

She ran,
free,
liberated,
and saved

Freedom

One by one,
skeletons crumbling
and tumbling down,
scattered dust beneath
my feet, no longer
smothering or stifling
me, my lips once sewn
to secrecy, slowly
dissolving and opening
up to all the hypocrisy,
no longer bonded or
mummified, caved in,
or made to justify,
as I danced around
for all to see the
weight has lifted
that was made for
me, and now I'm
celebrating to
eternity

Queen She

I'm not going to apologize
for being me, embracing this
smooth brown covering that
I so graciously own, and just
the mere glance of my
reflection sends chills
up my spine, knowing
that I Am that Prize

Irreplaceable

It's been awhile since I let loose,
letting my hair flow, like the way
I move, invincible, and definitely
irreplaceable

Rejoicing

Joy
ain't nothing like it,
after you fought your
way through the storm,
a little bruised, but
stronger, more resilient,
and more whole
in the end

That Feeling

I'm flying high today,
smiling and loving
every bit coming
my way

Get Up

Get up I say
Don't you dare
shut down
Don't you dare
stand still
Don't you dare,
I say
Don't you dare

Dazzling

Wake up sunshine,
beaming brighter
than any light I
know, sparkling
and displaying
that ray of hope

The Gathering

Today I had an epiphany,
that I was surrounded by
all who cared for me,
always alone and in
despair, not thinking
a soul cared until
they gathered in
harmony, surrounding
and embracing me, no
more weary or self pity,
that gathering really
redirected me

My Soul

Still is my heart,
my soul
Still is my life,
my time,
Frozen,
and captivated
at the same time,
as peace
swallows me
whole and
calms my
soul

Sheliah M. Callahan

Refuge

The desert sand,
Egyptian land,
take me whole
as I am

The Promise

Jesus softly tells me so,
a promised life, a wounded
soul, surrendered and defeated
at the throne

Sheliah M. Callahan

Escape

It's something about a roaring fire that puts
me at peace, more like a trance, as I watch
the flames do their dance, jumping all
around, and hearing crackling in the
background ever so faintly, but
loud enough to wipe out the noise
buzzing all around me, as deep
feelings suddenly become still,
fading away, and no longer
allowing it to dock or harbor
inside me, as I slip away,
mesmerized, and no
longer enticed by the
slightest things that
once engulfed me

The Battle

The battle is over,
rest assured,
far too long
I held on

To Dream

The scariest part of life
is having the courage
to go after a dream,
the courage to never
let go, the courage to
take hold, be bold,
and take control

The Finale

When the noise has stopped and memories
no longer linger on, it's the universe
telling me I have moved on, I have
healed, I have reached that point
of no more restless nights, for
my mind is now slumbering
and no longer wondering,
allowing the night to
rescue me, holding
and renewing me

Sheliah M. Callahan

Hidden

She comes,
sometimes camouflaged,
and at times moving like
the wind, and never quite
fitting in

Set Free

She looked different today,
painted in vibrant colors and
on display, illuminating this
energy felt by others, as she
glided by, joyous, and carefree,
and beaming like she was just
released, and set free

Peace I

No ripples
No waves
Still waters

Forgiving
Releasing
Evolving

Loving,
Accepting
and Freeing

Peace II

No ripples,
no waves
stillness
consumes me

Regrets moved on,
no longer hanging on

Then came forgiveness
that lifted me up,
freedom had come,
no sound,
just stillness
swallowed me up

Stagnate

Funny how life circles back,
repeating the past, and for
some reason no one seems
to understand this merry-
go-round, or perhaps
it's just others reverting
back to what they're use
to, their comfort zone, and
then wondering why life has
not come around their way,
to brighten their days with
their stagnate ways

For Me

Not today,
today is reserved
for me, not caring
how selfish it may
be, especially days
on end, caring for
others, while scurrying
around trying to make
their day complete

Finding Strength

Sometimes I wonder how strong I am,
and can I withstand the storms that
seem to follow me wherever I go,
as I struggle along trying to get
back to that place I know, where
I'm settled and familiarity often
soothes me as opposed to
venturing out, the unknown,
and not quite sure what it
would do for my psyche
alone when it has been
confused, and not sure
what is truth, or even
where to begin, or
should I even
retreat until then…

Finding Peace

That moment when stillness overtakes you,
and everything around you slows down,
silence surrounding you as serenity sets
in paralyzing every part of you, even
your thoughts that once haunted you,
and now surrendering, this energy
brewing has overtaken you, and
created this peacefulness, that is
now a part of you

Division

I wonder if my past has kept me from drowning, or falling in, as I wrap myself in a world that no one sees, or cares to fit in

I wonder as time passes, if my purpose was to simply exist, or perhaps take something from a place misunderstood, a place where others fail to coexist, because differences do exist

I wonder in a world divided, will unity prevail, allowing the younger ones to soar, taking the reins, as they lay out the world as they see fit

Celebration

How's this day treating you?
the sun is beaming and shining
on you, and that morning breeze
is breathing life into you, from
the crystal blue skies to the
clouds alone, setting this
picturesque scene, that
serene feeling pulsating
within me, and making
me wanna shimmy all
through the
streets,
oh what a joyous feeling,
pure laughter in the air,
a celebration, and
anticipation of what
this day will bring,
not only for you,
and me, but all the
people around us
too, that are
dancing, and
prancing, and
feeling liberated
in the streets

Sheliah M. Callahan

Hear Me

Speak to me,
let it flow,
no shield,
just bare,
and ready to reveal,
like a river running
over, and obstacles
invisible, pent-up
emotions shoot
out in the atmosphere,
mending and repairing,
accepting and releasing,
in order to start living

Save Me

Hurricanes come and go, fierce and relentless,
rattling, and shaking at times uncontrollably,
as I fight back, taking control, to see, to feel,
and praying that I never let go, as my breathing
becomes steady and more in control, weary at
times, but fighting to stay alive, fighting to
be seen, to be heard, and to be felt, and at
times just wanting others to believe in
me, simply take a chance on me, to
lift me when I Can No Longer
withstand these violent
storms, powerful, and
destructive, trying over
and over again to suck
me in, thrashing me
all around, while trying
to erase and destroy all
that I am, as I try to rise
and not allow these hurricanes
to take hold or take me by surprise,
Please,
Please
help me before I fold and finally…let go

Colored Glass

Looking back on what I thought love was,
was like looking through a rose colored
glass, blurry and unable to clearly see,
but hanging on to that sliver of hope,
that splendor of light, like being
trapped in a Kaleidoscope, not
quite what it appeared to be,
but magically seeing
what suited me, until
I was able to be
strong and move on

Uplifting

It's times like this that I let go, extending myself, and freeing myself, not only for me, but for you too

I rise in spite of……
I rise in spite of……
I rise in spite of……
It's times like this when I feel closed in, boxed in, and about to give in

Survival

Surrendering

In the end I'm all I have,
as the day goes by and the
night falls, the softness
of the moonlight
graciously warms
my soul, while
drifting and
surrendering
as my eyes
close

Surviving the Pain

My past hurts have only made
me stronger, and made me
want to climb the highest
mountains, freeing
myself, being one
with myself, and
loving myself

Sometimes

Sometimes my thoughts sail away,
casting out to never come back again

Sometimes my thoughts immobilize me,
blinding me to what I thought I knew

Sometimes my thoughts are musical,
jumping around, the highs and the lows

And sometimes my thoughts surface,
birthing life into the world, connecting,
historical, and phenomenal

Flying High

The feeling of being free, and opening up to all that's
coming to me, feeling untouchable, but more like an
angel, non-judgmental, and ridicule out the window,
and this feeling overcoming me, putting me at peace,
is a place I've never been before, but if this is what
it feels like, I accept that, I get that, I want that,
and I'm here to stay, not looking another way,
as I plant my roots, thanking God for this day

Not Amused

How will I greet you today?
Not quite seeing you the same,
and not quite sure which way
I'll sway, while feeling split
and not amused, and really
not caring to engage, or
entertain your ways

Sunday Blues

Can I simply be,
hidden and left
alone, and not
preached at
on this fine
Sunday
Morning

Sheliah M. Callahan

Survival

She lied to survive,
and sugarcoated her
reality with a cherry
on top as she muddled
through, for everyone
to see, and to even
make herself believe

Freeing Myself

Into the night I snuck away,
fleeing to save what was left
of me, leaving it all behind,
memories buried to never
surface or see daylight
again, for I found my
will to move on, and
this strength carried
me, freed me, and
reassured me

Unapologetic

I am boisterous, opinionated,
intelligent, black, and beautiful,
and to not to be mistaken,
misguided, blindsided,
or ignored as if I
never existed,
or just didn't
matter

The Past

I remember long ago,
whatever worries crept in,
blew with the wind, freeing
myself and allowing me to
surrender without culpability
and shamefulness, or the
feelings of being conflicted
of those who were against me,
or never understood my past
sufferings.

Difference in Us

A picture perfect canvas,
spread as far as I can see,
stars dangling precisely
where they need to be,
like ornaments hanging
from a tree, and that
feeling like one was
made perfectly for
me, sparkling that
shine, and intricately
made, just like
you and me

Cleansing

Something about the rain,
that cleanses and washes
all the pain away

Immersing My Soul

That feeling you get when that buzz
is no longer surrounding you, or trying
to break you, and with each beat, and
every breath, you hold on to that
moment, not wanting it to fade,
while immersing yourself, and
every part of you, as if you
were at the alter giving
all of you

Jewel

Letting go allows me to reconnect,
a jewel once hidden, now resurfacing,
and feeling life all over again

Wisdom

With no regrets, and with age comes
wisdom, or at least that moment
when you realized all you did
was live your best life under
the circumstances you were
given, and embraced at
that time

Silence

There're times when I question
my own existence, as others
around me gain their wings,
some gone way too soon
with no explanation, or
justification, and this
unspoken silence
consumes me, not
allowing me to
breath, feel, or
wanting to see
another day

Losing Myself

Succumbing to my worst days
bottled up into one

Restless

I'm tired of fighting
day after day,
day in, and
day out

Last Days

Let me say this and let's be clear,
I have seen my darkest days,
blinded and smothered, and
gasping for air, thinking it
was my last breath,
my last hour,
my last minute
and my
last second…

Sacrificing Me

I'm tired of making sacrifices,
making myself uncomfortable,
always appeasing, and not
once taking care of me

There're times when I don't
know how to settle myself,
always on the go, and not
even remembering how I
got from one point to the
other and then back home

Taking care of me is always
an afterthought, I guess
that's the mother in me,
ain't nothing right until
a mother's work is
complete

Clear to Me

It's so clear to me what you can't
see or feel when it comes to me,
could it be my presence, or am
I overshadowing you, or perhaps
overwhelming you, your ego not
releasing you, or could it be my
confidence, my joy, or the simple
fact that I'm magnetic and easy
for others to gravitate to, as
they admire my confidence,
style, and acknowledge all
that I do

Realization

Your misfortune will not be my burden,
your pain will not be for me to carry
when you created this world, sucked
me in, air tight, and I was unable to
escape, as I desperately tried to
find my way, to breath again,
and to no longer suffocate
under your crippling ways

Masterpiece

Telling my story releases me,
it's kind of like painting a
masterpiece, outlining my
beginning, with splashes
of colors depicting my
trials and tribulations,
from sadness, to pain,
to misfortunes, and
then to a life
opening up
again

I sigh,

as the restraints
slowly melt away,
and a masterpiece
is made, not only
for the world to
see, but for me
to receive and
accept all that
has made me

Blessings from Above

God has blessed me
in every way, from
sun up to sun down,
and protected me
along the way

Welcome Home

These four walls surrounding me, closing in on me,
have never been home to me when my soul was
shredded and not complete, internally shackled,
with no release, bringing me no peace, or any
type of resolution that I could clearly see, and
traveling the world to find that place, that
space, to fill this void that has been dead
to me, and at times drifting, feeling so
surreal, while letting go, and releasing
that pain to the northern winds, encased
and frozen, to never come back again,
as I battle this hatred taking over me,
from years of racism surrounding
me, crippling, choking, and stripping
me whole, as I cry out to the world,
as one we gather, as one we stand,
that perfect rainbow, and finally
finding that peace from within,
lovingly embracing all of me,
giving myself grace and you
too, as I'm feeling full and
whole again, which is exactly
where I need to be, and what
represents home to me

A New Day

Darkness looming, clouds descending,
and hailing, and winds uncovering once
again, but then spring mounts and comes
crashing in always at the tail end, with
sprinkles of mist clearing the way,
while leaving behind those chilly
ways, for a more vibrant and
colorful type of day

ACKNOWLEDGEMENTS

This body of work has been a long time coming. Expressing myself has allowed me to be free, and to give myself permission to be me. So many thanks to be given along the way to family and friends for their support and encouragement.

Beth, my dear friend, thank you for all your support and for editing, and assisting me in bringing my ideas to life.

Julie, thank you for your kindness over the years, and for providing your expertise in the editing phase.

Deborah B., Glynis, Kim, Paula, Regina, Rhonda, and Tanyel, thank you for your friendship, love, and encouragement over the years.

My parents, Ray and Corine, thank you for always supporting me, loving me unconditionally, and instilling confidence in me.

To my dear brother, Ray Jr., who keeps me laughing, and has always found humor in everything, regardless of what life throws at you.

To my significant other, Raymond, thank you for being my safe place that allows me to be authentic and feel free, and open to love again.

To my dear son, Brandon, my greatest accomplishment. Thank you for your patience and for graciously listening to my poems throughout the years. You have so many talents and so much to offer. Keep being you, and embrace all that you are, just as I have.

ABOUT THE AUTHOR

Sheliah Callahan grew up in Southern California and had a love for writing and expressing herself from an early age. Sheliah received her degree in psychology from California State University, San Bernardino, and worked with children and families for over 25 years before retiring. In her spare time she enjoys traveling and spending time with family and friends.

www.ingramcontent.com/pod-product-compliance
Lightning Source LLC
LaVergne TN
LVHW010346070526
838199LV00065B/5795